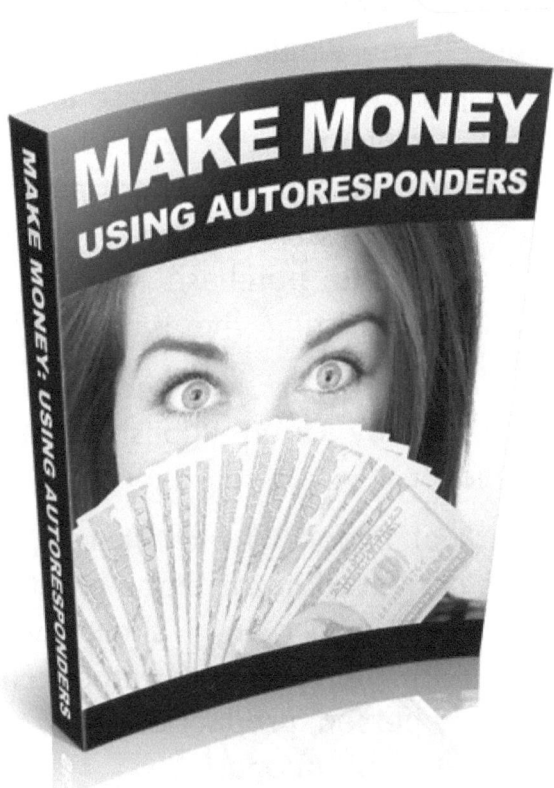

Make Money Using Autoresponders

Thomas Rutledge

ISBN 978-1-105-06738-9

©2012

Wedelivertraffic.info

Copyright

directly or indirectly. While every effort has been made to ensure reliability and accuracy of the information within, all liability, negligence or otherwise, from any use, misuse or abuse of the operation of any methods, strategies, instructions or ideas contained in the material herein, is the sole responsibility of the reader.

Any copyrights not held by publisher are owned by their respective authors.

All information is generalized, presented for informational purposes only and presented "as is" without warranty or guarantee of any kind.

Any trademarks and brands referred to in this book are for illustrative purposes only, are the property of their respective owners and not affiliated with this publication in any way. Any trademarks are being used without permission, and the publication of the trademark is not authorized by, associated with or sponsored by the trademark owner.

ISBN 978-1-105-06738-9

Table of Contents

Wedelivertraffic.info

Generating Traffic To Your Website

It's the critical ingredient in every successful online business's marketing strategy, and the one component that will make or break your ability to build a profitable business and make money online.

TRAFFIC!

But not just any traffic will do.

It's easy to go out and purchase "hits" from various traffic sources, in fact, within a few minutes you could chew up your website's bandwidth limit with these random visitors, but it will do very little for your bottom line.

What you really need are heavily targeted prospects, not visitors. You need to reach deep into your market and funnel in the hungriest crowds of buyer's possible, so that you are able to maximize not only your outreach, but also the overall profitability of your online business.

After all, it makes absolutely no sense if you are able to generate 50,000 visitors if none of these people are genuinely interested in the types of products or services you are offering.

We need to flood our websites with targeted traffic that are genuinely interested in our offers, and who will become part of our customer base.

Relevant, targeted – and active traffic that will power our business and fuel our marketing campaigns!

So, the question is; how do you get your share?

There are hundreds of different ways to generate traffic to your website. From search engine optimization, to feeder site resources, to pay per click marketing and sponsorship opportunities, there is no shortage of opportunities available to you.

Setting up your traffic system and finally being able to claim your share of unlimited traffic from free online resources requires a bit of time and effort on your part, but once you've completed the process and set the wheels into motion, you'll benefit from a system that is designed to work quickly and efficiently, and over the long haul.

Are you ready to get started? Let's begin!

Top 5 Ways To Generate Low Cost Website Traffic

There is one hard and fast rule in generating income for your website: A steady flow of website traffic. If no one goes to your site, it hardly bares a chance of generating an income. Many sites have tried and failed in doing so, and these results to the sites demise. It takes money to maintain an income generating site; it also takes money to make money.

BUT, it doesn't take a whole caboodle of cash to generate website traffic for your site.

Ever wonder how does big hit sites drive traffic top their site? Most of them are spending tons of money to drive the traffic to their sites, investing in many advertising campaigns and different forms of marketing schemes and gimmickries. This is all worthwhile because, well, they are what they are now, high earning, big hitting websites.

You don't have to do this if you don't really have their resources. There are many ways to generate low cost website traffic without having to spend what you don't have or can't afford. Many people have banked on high cost methods and have ended up losing their shirt over it.

Here I present to you the Top five ways to generate low cost website traffic that could help your site a whole lot. Even if you only get a small percentage of successful visitors in to client ratio it still works especially if you get a high number of website traffic.

Exchange Links

This is a sure and proven method. Rarely would you see a site where there is no link to another site. Many webmasters are willing to exchange links with one another so that they could produce more public awareness about their sites. You'll soon see and feel the sudden upsurge of the traffic coming in to your site from other sites.

A major prerequisite in exchanging links with other sites is having the same niche or content as the other site. They should share a common subject so that there is continuity in the providing of service and information to what interests your target traffic.

Exchanging links also boosts your chances of getting a high ranking in search engine results. It is common knowledge that search engines ranks high sites that have in-bound and out-bound theme-related links. With a good ranking position in the search engines, you will generate more traffic in your website without the high costs.

Traffic Exchange

This is like exchanging links but on a different higher level. This may cost a bit more than exchanging or trading links but could be made cheaper because you get to earn credits. You can use those credits when viewing others traffic, while you earn credits when someone views yours.

Traffic exchange services are the viewing of another's site or page. This is done vice versa where a site can use your sites contents and so can you to his or her site. You both benefit from each others efforts to generate traffic. The other sites visitors can go to your pages and know more about your site as well as theirs. Once again the public awareness of your sites existence is boosted.

Write and Submit Articles

There are many e-zines and online encyclopedias in the internet which provides free space for articles to be submitted. If you want to save costs, you can do the articles yourself. There are many freelance writers who are willing to write for you for a small fee, but to save money, it is wise to do those articles yourself.

Write articles that are themed along with the niche of your site. Write something that you have expertise on so that when they read it, they can feel your knowledge about the subject and will be eager to go to your site. Write articles that produce tips and guidelines to the subject or niche your site has.

Include a resource box at the end of your article that can link them to your site. Write a little about yourself and your site. If you provide a light,

---

information-laden and interesting article, they will go to your site for more.

Make a Newsletter

This may sound like hard work because of all the articles you may need to use to build a newsletter but on the contrary, this is not so. There are many writers and sites that are willing to provide free articles as long as they can get their name in on your newsletter. This will also provide free advertising for them as well.

As your newsletter gets pass around, you can widen your public awareness and build an opt-in list that can regularly visit your site.

Join Online Communities and Forums

This only requires your time and nothing else. You can share your knowledge and expertise with many online communities as well as your website. You can get free advertising when you go to forums that have the same subject or niche with your site.

Share your two cents and let them see how knowledgeable you are with the subject. As you build your reputation, you also build the reputation of your site, making it a reputable and honest business that could be frequented and trusted by many people.

Getting Started With Autoresponders

If you've just started your online business or decided to get into affiliate marketing, you'll be looking to make money. Making money on the net with your new business can be a little tricky, unless you have an autoresponder. An autoresponder is the ideal way to carry out your day to day business – saving yourself quite a bit of time and money.

If you don't have a lot of money to spend, there are places on the Internet where you can get an autoresponder for free. Keep in mind that if you don't purchase your autoresponder, the free ones normally come with downsides. The most common downside to free autoresponders will be the ads on your emails, which will more than likely send your customers the wrong idea.

When you get your autoresponder, the first thing you'll need to do is set it up with messages or articles that relate to your business. This way, when you send out emails or messages, you'll be sending out material that relates to your business or products. You should try to write some of your own if you can, which will help you get started in the right direction.

When you load up your autoresponder, you should try to load it with at least 52 messages. This way, you'll something to send for each week of the year. If you have trouble loading your autoresponder with this many messages or articles, there are places online where you can get your material for free. If you simply don't have the time, you can always start with a few messages then go back and add more at a later time.

Once you have your autoresponder preloaded with messages or articles, you'll need to set up your signature. Your signature will be displayed at the bottom of every message your autoresponder sends, and should be your name and link to your business. You can also add a short description of your business as well, which will let clients or interested customers know a bit of information about your business. Your name and link to your business will go a long way, letting your customers know that you are professional.

Once you have everything set up, all you need to do is start sending out emails. Your autoresponder can be set up to send messages automatically. You can also send out emails daily, weekly, or monthly if you prefer. Almost all autoresponders are flexible, easy to use, and will send out your messages when you decide. Once your subscriber list starts to build up, and you get more email addresses to your autoresponder, you'll quickly see that it's very beneficial. After you have used your autoresponder a few months – you won't be able to imagine your business without it.

Email Autoresponders

Those of you who wish to take control of your business on the Internet with automated tasks need a functional and easy to use automatic email response system. An automatic email response system will take care of any emails you receive, and automatically deliver a response to potential clients 24 hours a day – 7 days a week.

You can set up your autoresponder program on your own computer or server without any problems. Using your own program is the way to go, especially if you want to avoid paying a monthly fee to companies that charge for the same services. There are several companies out there that offer autoresponder services, although they can get expensive over time.

If you decide to use your own email autoresponder program, you can save a lot of money and a lot of time. These programs will streamline your business, freeing up your time to concentrate on other important areas. You can let your email program handle responses and follow up emails, while you work on making other ideas work or just getting out there and spending time with your family.

An email autoresponder can help you generate thousands of leads in little to no time at all. With a lot of leads, comes money. Although you may disagree, a customer list is what leads to money. If you don't have a customer list or database, chances are that you won't be doing a lot of sales. Having customers to send emails and products to is a plus – especially when you weigh in the fact that customers make your business. Without customers, you wouldn't make any money at all.

When you are using an autoresponder with your website, you should always include a subscription box for visitors who wish to sign up. This way, anyone who visits your website and wishes to learn more about your products or offers, can easily sign up. Your autoresponder will instantly send out an email, which will in turn help you build your customer list. To survive in the online world of business, you'll need to have a customer list. Autoresponders will help you manage your list and help it grow at the same time.

Choosing Your Autoresponder Software

It can be a somewhat difficult and time consuming task to find the right autoresponder. There are a lot of choices available on the Internet, each one ranging in price and features. Before you decide to purchase your own autoresponder, you should first think about your budget as well as your requirements. This way, you'll know what you want and how much you are willing to spend.

First, you'll need to decide the features you want. Next, you'll need to take a look at some of the different types of autoresponders available on the market. You'll also need to decide which type is right for you, and which brand name you think would work the best. You can answer these questions by comparing different brands, prices, features, and licensing restrictions.

For a business, autoresponders can be great. As most of us already know, autoresponders are programs that will send out an automated response via email to a specified address. In most cases, the response you get back from an email autoresponder is short and sweet, normally letting you know that someone is on vacation, away from their computer, or that they have received your message.

The only real problem to autoresponders is the fact that they will replay to any email that they receive. If you are subscribed to a mailing list and used your autoresponder address to sign up, it can easily create a problem. Anytime someone sends you an email to

Wedelivertraffic.info

your responder address it will send an automated reply. It can also lack important features that you need to follow up on your clients or subscribers as well.

For the Internet marketing guru, there are sequential autoresponders. These types of autoresponders are designed to collect different email addresses then send out a variety of pre determined messages through email to subscribers that you have on your list. If you have a sequential autoresponder and use it correctly, it can help you bring back more visitors. It can be a very handy tool to have around, especially if you work with a lot of clients. It can help you keep track of subscribers, as well as keep them informed about what is going on with your business.

All across the Internet there are many types of autoresponders. They range from web based programs to scripts or programs that run through your computer or personal server. An autoresponder will be a major part of your online business, which is why you should always put forth the time and effort to find the best one for your money. If you put the proper research and time into finding your ideal autoresponder, you'll save yourself a lot of time and headache in the long run.

Basically, there are three main types of autoresponders that you can choose from – remote hosted, locally hosted, and desktop hosted. Remote hosted are hosted on someone else's server or website. Locally hosted will allow you to work programs for your own web server. Desktop programs on the other hand, will allow you to work from your own computer. Most people choose to go with locally hosted, as it makes things a lot easier.

Before you decide on which type of autoresponder to purchase, you should make sure that you understand what each type will offer you. There are a variety of autoresponders to choose from, meaning that some may not offer what you need. You can always research each type, and then compare prices and features. This way, you'll know which type of autoresponder will work the best for your needs as well as your business.

Researching Auto Responders

If you are in the Internet marketing business or if you run a business online, an autoresponder can make a world of difference. They can handle a majority of your technical support questions and informational requests, by sending out automated messages to interested customers. When they get an email, they will respond instantly with a preset message. This can save you quite a bit of time- especially if you get a lot of emails on a daily basis.

Out there on the Internet, there are many autoresponders to choose from. They are classified into three main types – locally hosted, remote hosted and desktop hosted. Each type has pros and cons, depending on your needs. Locally and desktop hosted programs will give you complete control over the program, as you run them through your own server or website. Remote hosted on the other hand, is ran through a third party service provider. Remote programs cost you a monthly fee, while desktop and locally hosted programs cost one fee – then you have complete ownership of the program.

Before you decide to purchase an autoresponder, you should always compare and see what each one has to offer you. If you are interested in running one from your server or website, then you'll need to look at desktop and locally hosted autoresponders. There are free programs available online, although they will normally come with strings attached, such as ads in your emails. This can be a bad thing, as ads in your email will give customers the wrong impression. www.Automatic-Responder.com is a great service that also offers a free version for up to 250 subscribers and no advertisements.

When you purchase one of these types of autoresponder programs, you should always research and find out all that you can. There are many programs out there that you can buy, many of which will offer you great features at a great price. Buying your program is the way to go, especially if you have an image to uphold. Once you have found a program and buy it, it will be yours for as long as you decide to use it.

If you are looking towards a remotely hosted autoresponder, you'll need to research for the best prices and service, this is a must when shopping around. You'll be dealing with a company who has control over the address of the autoresponder, meaning that your domain name won't appear in the emails you send using the autoresponder. This can be good for some, although many prefer to have their name in their emails.

When it all comes down to it, you should always research an autoresponder before you decide to make a purchase or use a free program. There are several out there to choose from, although some are far superior to others. If you take the time and research what each one has to offer you and how much it will cost you – you'll end up with an autoresponder that will prove to be more than worth the cost.

Boosting Business with Autoresponders

These days, most everyone is familiar with an autoresponder, although many don't know why they are beneficial to businesses. If you aren't familiar with autoresponders, you would probably find yourself amazed with them. An autoresponder can help your business by automatically emailing your clients and customers with a preset message that will help to increase your sales.

An autoresponder can help your list of clients grow, even send each one of them their own personalized email message. If you choose, you can also follow up each individual email with repeated emails, varying the content whenever you wish. These programs will also allow you to keep track of conversations, and send out broadcast email messages whenever you have news or new products to offer your clients.

As research in the past has shown, personalized email from autoresponders is a great way to boost your business. When you send a personalized email to one of your clients, the autoresponder by can address him or her by their name – which always makes a customer take notice. While you could do this yourself using traditional email, it could take you a few hours if you have a long list of customers.

Autoresponders make sending personalized email a snap. All you need to do is set up your email template, then select where you like the name to go.

You can add everyone in your customer list to the autoresponder, which makes sending emails a snap. Once you have everything ready to go, all you need to do is send out the emails with one simple click. Best of all – you don't have to set it up again when you need to send out broadcast messages.

Although there are some people who will buy products after one or two emails, most people require about seven or eight emails before they will purchase anything. Autoresponders can really help you there, as they will do all of the emailing for you. You don't have to keep sending manual emails or anything like that. All you need to do is set up the email address, type in your preset message, and then feel free to send it as many times as you like.

Through the use of an autoresponder you can really boost your business. If you run an Internet marketing business, this tool will prove to be invaluable. You can spend less time sending messages – and more time doing what you enjoy. If you've never tried an autoresponder before, you owe it yourself to check out everything they will do for you and your business. Online businesses can get a lot of emails on a daily basis – which is where the autoresponder will really start to shine and show you just how great of an asset it really is.

Build Interest with Autoresponder Messages

If you are using your autoresponder to sell a product or service, you must be very careful as to how you approach your potential customer. Few people like a hard sale, and marketers have known for years that in most cases, a prospect must hear your message an average of seven times before they will make a purchase. How do you accomplish this with autoresponders?

It's really quite simple, and in fact, the autoresponders make getting the message to your potential customers those seven times possible. On the Internet, without the use of autoresponders, you probably could not achieve that. Too often, marketers make the mistake of literally slamming the potential customer with a hard sales pitch with the first autoresponder message – this won't work.

You build interest slowly. Start with an informative message – a message that educates the reader in some way on the topic that your product or service is related to. At the bottom of the message, include a link to the sales page for your product. Use that first message to focus on the problem that your product or service can solve, with just a hint of the solution.

Build up from there, moving into how your product or service can solve a problem, and then with the next message, ease into the benefits of your product – giving the reader more actual information with each and every message. Your final message should be the sale pitch – not your first one! With each message, make sure that you are giving the customer information pertaining to the topic – free information! This is what will keep them interested in what you have to say.

This type of marketing is an art. It may take time to get it exactly right. Use the examples that other marketers have set for you. Pay attention to the messages that you receive from other marketers. Start a 'swap' file, and keep those messages. Use some of the better sales copy for your own autoresponder messages – just make sure that yours doesn't turn out to be an exact copy of someone else's sales message!

Remember not to start with a hard sale. Build your potential customers interest. Keep building on what the problem is, and how your product or service can solve that problem or fill that need. If you are doing this right, by the time the potential customer reads the last message in that series, they will be convinced enough to make a purchase!

Increasing Your Sales with Autoresponders

The autoresponder is without a doubt one of the best marketing tools you can get. It is a widely used application that will automatically respond to any email that it receives. They are considered to be magical indeed, triggered by a blank email that they receive to their address. Once they receive this email, they automatically start working for your business.

Whenever someone sends the autoresponder a message, the individual who sent the message will receive a preset email message with the information they were seeking. Depending on the servers and speed of the Internet, the email response will happen very fast. Autoresponders have always been known for their quick speed and fast responses to any type of email message they receive.

One of the best things about autoresponders is the fact that they are always available. They are always there 24/7, providing your clients and customers with the information they seek. They will make your business life easier, by boosting your sales. They require little work from you, yet they are easy to operate. They can also make managing your customers and clients easier than ever, as they will help you keep track of your responses and keep up with email addresses you receive.

Even if you've never used an autoresponder before, you can easily use it to your advantage with your online business. You can pre-set it to say a variety of messages, even inform your clients about future offers and products. This is a great way to get your message out there, especially if you are currently holding a sale or other deal that you know people won't want to miss out on. Autoresponders will work for you day or night, making your company information available to anyone whenever they want it.

Contrary to popular belief, not all buyers are impulse buyers. Research has shown that less than 15% of those who visit websites are impulse buyers. Although most websites focus themselves on getting visitors to buy their products immediately, most buyers need time to think about a product or offer they will purchase it. Most buyers don't like to buy something immediately, simply because they may not be familiar with the product or know what it can do for them. Therefore, most buyers will learn all they can about something before they decide to go ahead and purchase it.

You can also use an autoresponder to distribute courses, articles or reports to your clients and subscribers. They are also great for providing free information to interested individuals, or immediately sending out information about your products and opportunities. You can also choose to send out price lists as well, or welcome new clients to your organization. If customers have purchased from you before, you can use an autoresponder to send out confirmations, thank you notes, and even offer discounts to those who buy your products.

In the world of Internet marketing, autoresponders are simply beneficial to have. They are worth more than the price you pay for them, simply because they will provide you with so much for so little. One of the best in the business is www.Automatic-Responder.com. Sending out information is easy with an autoresponder – as it will provide information about your company and products to interested clients the instant they need it.

All in all, an autoresponder will help you operate your business easier than ever before. Unlike other programs you can get for your online business, autoresponders will keep you in a constant state of readiness. You can feel free to go out and do what you want – and rest assured that your autoresponder will be there to supply information to those who need it.

Give Potential Customers a Preview with Autoresponders

Building customer interest and excitement is the first step to successfully marketing many products. Autoresponders play a vital role in building this interest and excitement. For instance, if you were developing an ebook, you may want to start telling your website visitors and opt-in subscribers about it. Start building interest; tell them what this product will do for them, and how soon it will be available. Do more than build interest by telling them about it. Use an autoresponder to let them preview your product! Even though you will be selling the product, you can allow your potential customers to preview the information. Have you ever seen previews for movies that will be playing in theaters soon? It is the same concept.

Load one chapter of the ebook into an autoresponder, and put a form on your website where your visitors can enter their name and email address to receive the preview chapter free of charge. This gets their name on your list of potential customer. Each week, send a reminder email, letting them know how close the release date is, and what they can expect from your product – keep building interest and excitement.

Finally, a couple of days before you are ready to launch your product offer those that received the preview the option to buy a pre-release copy. You can opt to offer a discounted price, or leave the pricas it will be on launch day – the choice is yours.

Take a look at the list of people who signed up to receive the preview. How many of them are still 'subscribed' to that list? They've had the option to stop receiving notices about your product, but they chose to keep receiving the information you were sending. These are highly targeted prospects for your product. They have already shown you that they have an interest in your product, and a large number of those people are simply waiting on the autoresponder broadcast message that will let them know that it is time to pick up their copy of your product!

Isn't automation a wonderful thing? Using an autoresponder, you are able to see how much of a market there is for your product, and build a great deal of interest in it before it is ever released. This is the key to making sales on launch day. Use autoresponders to build the interest. Get your prospects excited about what is about to come – and on launch day, give them what they are waiting for and watch the sales pour in!

Writing Follow Up Messages for Autoresponders

When it comes to making a sell using your autoresponder, follow up messages are very important. Most website visitors won't buy something on the first visit; it normally takes more than 6 or 7 visits before they decide to make a purchase. To keep them interested and eventually make the sale, you'll need to come up with some innovative yet captivating follow up messages.

When you start writing your message, you'll need to come up with compelling headlines. Compelling headlines will draw attention from readers, making them feel excited to read the rest of your message. If you send a message with a shoddy headline, chances are that your readers will just glance over the email and not pay much attention to it at all.

You can also grab attention from your readers by sending them personalized messages with their names and other details. There are several autoresponders that personalize messages through the insertion of codes. When you send a message out, the code is replaced with the personal information of the subscriber. When receiving the email, the reader will see his or her personal information instead of the code.

The first message that you send out is normally an introduction message. This message should be geared towards giving readers what to expect from your messages. You can also mention information about your company and your products as well. Your introduction message is very important, as it sets the pace for the messages that follow.

When you send out your second message, you should inform readers about your products and services. Make sure that you explain what your products do and how your readers can benefit from using them. Then, in the messages that follow, you should put added emphasis on your services and products. You should be trying to convince readers that they simply must have your products and that your products are a cut above the rest.

To ensure that you get a sale, you should include comparisons between what you offer and what competitors offer. This way, you'll show potential customers that you are indeed the best, with the best features and the best prices. Once you have a few satisfied customers, you'll start to build up your credibility. If a customer is satisfied, he will let you and others know. Once a customer has praised your products, you can add it to a testimonial and send it out in a future follow up message.

When you end a message, make sure that you leave a teaser for the next message. This way, your customers will look forward to receiving your next message. You should also carefully weave in messages regarding your contact and order information as well, so readers can place an order without any problems. If you put some time and thought into your follow up messages – you'll start racking up customers and sales in no time at all.

Autoresponders and Spam – What You Need To Know

There are laws against sending spam. There are even laws that you must adhere to when you send out email that was requested. No matter what type of email you are sending out, the chances are good that the anti-spam laws apply to you in some way.

In order to be in compliance with the anti-spam laws in various states in the US, each commercial email that you send must include your name or business name, your street address, city, state, zip code, and phone number. You must also include instructions that will allow the recipient to remove themselves from your mailing list. If you fail to do any of this, you are essentially breaking the law in various states – no matter what state or country you live in!

Protect yourself from spam complaints in any way that you can. Make sure that when a customer requests any type of information from you that an email is sent requesting confirmation before any other email is sent. If someone is placing an order from you, include a check box on the order form, asking for permission to send them periodic emails. Never use your autoresponder to send unsolicited commercial email!

Making The Most Of Autoresponders

If you've created a website and started adding your content to it, chances are you've also built some links and submitted some articles to the major search engines. After you have done all of the above, the next logical step, which many happen to overlook, is to take your business to the next level with an autoresponder. These tools are great to have, although many simply overlook them.

Often times, someone will visit your website through a link or search engine. In many cases, a potential buyer will look around your site and find exactly what he has been looking for. Sometimes, the buyer will get distracted with other things, and leave the site before he makes a purchase. There are many reasons as to why a potential buyer might leave your site on accident before making a purchase, although you can capitalize and make the most of this opportunity with the use of an autoresponder.

By capturing the visitor's email address, an autoresponder will give you the chance to contact the potential buyer in the future and capitalize on the sale that you missed out on before. Although autoresponders are mostly known for their abilities to automatically answer email, they are also more flexible, allowing you to do so much more. If you use your autoresponder creatively and productively, you'll gain more leads and customers than you ever imagined.

The best autoresponders out there will manage your customer list and continue to follow up with customers who have signed up on your list. You can also keep your autoresponder list updated with new products and services as well. These programs will grow with you, allowing you to build a reputation in your area of business and become an expert over time.

Through the use of an autoresponder and an affiliate program you can contact your affiliates quickly and easily to let them know about new offers you have or offer them new material that they can use to help them sell your products to increase your sales and their commissions. You can also send out broadcast emails to your affiliates as well, providing them with tips and helpful advice that will assist them with selling your products.

Autoresponders are also a great way to provide advertising as well. If someone is interested in advertising on your website, you can use the autoresponder to automatically send out an email detailing the cost of advertising and how the individual can find out more about it as well. This is a great asset, especially if you make a lot of income with advertising on your website.

Another way you can make the most of your autoresponder is by allowing your visitors a taste of what you have to offer and the quality of your products or services. If you plan to send out samples, you should avoid making it appear to be a sales letter. If you do, you'll normally end up losing more business than you gain. Most buyers don't like receiving sales letters, and will avoid doing business with you if they receive a sales letter.

Even if you've never used an autoresponder before, you can find many different uses for it. Autoresponders are great for many different purposes, other than answering emails. There are several types to choose from as well, which gives you plenty of opportunities for your business. All you need to do is select the type that works best for you – then discover more and more creative ways to use it to your advantage.

Tracking Autoresponder Responses

As an Internet marketer, it is vitally important to know how well your advertising campaigns are doing.

Advertising campaigns cost a lot of time and money, and campaigns that are not doing well need to either be changed or scraped. When using autoresponders for purposes of Internet marketing, you will be able to tell how well your autoresponder messages are doing by using response tracking.

Autoresponder response tracking is usually easily set up with the higher quality paid autoresponder services. Using the tracking set up tool, you simply enter the web site address that you want your readers to visit, and the software generates a brand new URL. This URL is used track the number of clicks that you have from the autoresponder message to the website that you are promoting.

When a person clicks on that special URL, the click is captured, and they are automatically redirected to the website that you intended them to arrive at. The visitor does not know that they have been redirected in most cases. You can monitor the results through the control panel of your autoresponder service account. The control panel will tell you how many messages were delivered, and how many clicks were received. Most quality autoresponders will even include a feature that allows you to track how many of the emails were opened. This is a great marketing research tool for mass email marketing.

Not all autoresponder services offer tracking abilities such as this. If tracking is important to you, you need to make sure that this is one of the features of the autoresponder service before you sign up. This feature gives you the ability to know whether the message you are sending out is effective, or if changes need to be made. It also allows you to see if the sales copy on your website is effective, in a 'round-about' way. For instance, if you are getting thousands of clicks from the autoresponder message, but very few clicks from the sales page to the order page, you know that the autoresponder message is working, but the sales copy is failing.

If you have never tracked your autoresponder responses before, you should definitely consider it. Again, this information allows you to find out what is working, and what is not working. It will essentially make your autoresponder marketing much more effective and profitable. You will most likely be very surprised at the results of the tracking!

Writing Follow Up Messages For Autoresponders
When it comes to making a sell using your autoresponder, follow up messages are very important. Most website visitors won't buy something on the first visit; it normally takes more than 6 or 7 visits before they decide to make a purchase. To keep them interested and eventually make the sale, you'll need to come up with some innovative yet captivating follow up messages.

When you start writing your message, you'll need to come up with compelling headlines. Compelling headlines will draw attention from readers, making them feel excited to read the rest of your message. If you send a message with a shoddy headline, chances are that your readers will just glance over the email and not pay much attention to it at all.

You can also grab attention from your readers by sending them personalized messages with their names and other details. There are several autoresponders that personalize messages through the insertion of codes. When you send a message out, the code is replaced with the personal information of the subscriber. When receiving the email, the reader will see his or her personal information instead of the code.

The first message that you send out is normally an introduction message. This message should be geared towards giving readers what to expect from your messages. You can also mention information about your company and your products as well. Your introduction message is very important, as it sets the pace for the messages that follow.

When you send out your second message, you should inform readers about your products and services. Make sure that you explain what your products do and how your readers can benefit from using them. Then, in the messages that follow, you should put added emphasis on your services and products. You should be trying to convince readers that they simply must have your products and that your products are a cut above the rest.

To ensure that you get a sale, you should include comparisons between what you offer and what competitors offer. This way, you'll show potential customers that you are indeed the best, with the best features and the best prices. Once you have a few satisfied customers, you'll start to build up your credibility. If a customer is satisfied, he will let you and others know. Once a customer has praised your products, you can add it to a testimonial and send it out in a future follow up message.

When you end a message, make sure that you leave a teaser for the next message. This way, your customers will look forward to receiving your next message. You should also carefully weave in messages regarding your contact and order information as well, so readers can place an order without any problems. If you put some time and thought into your follow up messages – you'll start racking up customers and sales in no time at all.

Personalizing Autoresponders

Have you ever walked into a store in your town, and been addressed by name? This has probably happened to you at stores that you frequent often.

The shop owner knows your name, and uses it. He remembers you, and he wants you to know that he cared enough about you and your business to remember you. In the offline world, this is just one aspect of customer support.

Customer service like this is almost impossible to achieve on the Internet, but some semblance of it can exist when you personalize your autoresponder messages. Autoresponder messages can be set up to address people by their first or last name – or both.

In fact, there is quite a bit of personalized information that can be added, depending on the autoresponder that you are using.

The information is included in the autoresponder messages by using codes. Each autoresponder will use different codes to insert the information in your messages. You simply write your message, and put the codes where you want the personalized information to appear. For instance, your message may start out with 'Hello (code for first name)! In this case, the person's first name will be inserted where that code is.

Personalizing your autoresponder messages will most likely improve your response rate. Research has shown that emails that are personalized with the person's first name are opened more often, and those people are generally more receptive to the contents of the email message. It is usually very easy to do. You write one message, using the codes where you want the personalization, then, no matter who that one email is sent out to, their personal information will appear where the codes are.

Of course, the autoresponder must collect the information first. This is done with the use of forms that activate the autoresponder. For instance, if you are giving away a free ebook, and you have your visitor fill out a form with their email address to receive the download instructions for the ebook by email, that form should collect any type of information that you want for personalization – such as a first name, as well as the email address. If that information is not collected, the autoresponder won't have anything to insert where that code appears in your messages!

Take a look around the control panel of your autoresponder, and find out what type of personalization you can add to your autoresponder messages. You may be very surprised at the improved results!

www.ingramcontent.com/pod-product-compliance
Lightning Source LLC
Chambersburg PA
CBHW021850170526
45157CB00006B/2383